JNFJ

Festive Foods for the Holidays™

An Easter
Holiday
COOKBOOK

Emily Raabe

The Rosen Publishing Group's
PowerKids Press™
New York

The recipes in this cookbook
are intended for a child to make together with an adult.

Many thanks to Ruth Rosen and her test kitchen.

For Rachel, my favorite chef

Published in 2002 by The Rosen Publishing Group, Inc.
29 East 21st Street, New York, NY 10010

Copyright © 2002 by The Rosen Publishing Group, Inc.

First Edition

Book Design: Maria E. Melendez
Project Editor: Frances E. Ruffin

Photo Credits: Cover and title page (mother and daughter) © SuperStock; cover and title page (eggs, breads) © StockFood/Irvine; cover and title page (chocolate) © StockFood America/Eising; cover and title page (coconut, salt, pepper, pie, utensils, milk, cheese, ham, eggs, oil, jelly beans, sugar), p. 6 (deer) © Digital Stock; p. 6 (meadow) © Digital Vision; p. 9 © Bob Krist/CORBIS; p. 10 © StockFood America/Eising; p. 13 © AFP/CORBIS; p. 13 (inset) © Eric Kamp/Index Stock; p. 14 © Craig Aurness/CORBIS; p. 16 © Jacqui Hurst/CORBIS; p. 20, p. 20 (inset) © ASAP Ltd./Index Stock; page number design illustrated by Maria E. Melendez; all recipe photos by Arlan Dean.

Raabe, Emily.
An Easter holiday cookbook / Emily Raabe.
 p. cm. — (Festive foods for the holidays)
ISBN: 0-8239-5624-5
1. Easter cookery—Juvenile literature. [1. Easter. 2. Easter cookery. 3. Holidays. 4. Cookery, International.] I. Title. II. Series.
TX739.2.E37 R33 2002
641.5'68–dc21

00—012444

Manufactured in the United States of America

Contents

A Spring Feast

For people who belong to the **Christian** faith, Easter is the most important holiday of the year. At Easter, Christians remember their savior, Jesus Christ. Christians believe that Jesus was crucified, but that three days later he rose from the dead and went to heaven. Easter celebrates this miracle of Jesus' **rebirth** into heaven.

Easter does not fall on the same date every year. Instead, Christians **celebrate** Easter on the first Sunday after the first full moon of spring. Easter can be celebrated anytime between March 22 and April 25. Some Christians who live in Greece or Eastern Europe follow the **Orthodox** tradition of Christianity. They can celebrate Easter from one to five weeks after other Christians. At Easter, Greek people enjoy eating koulourakia cookies made with sesame seeds.

Greek Easter Cookies

You will need:
- ½ pound (227 g) butter
- ¾ cups (177 ml) sugar
- 1 teaspoon (5 ml) vanilla
- 2 eggs, separated
- 2 teaspoons (10 ml) baking powder
- 1 teaspoon (5 ml) baking soda
- 4 cups (946 ml) flour
- ½ cup (118 ml) buttermilk
- ½ cup (118 ml) sesame seeds

How to do it:

Have an adult help you set an oven at 350 degrees Fahrenheit (177 °C).

Melt the butter. Add sugar and vanilla.

Stir in the egg yolks, one at a time.

Add all of the remaining ingredients, and stir until blended.

Roll small pieces of dough into sticks of pencil width and 8 inches (20 cm) long.

For each cookie, twist two dough sticks into a braid.

Brush each cookie with egg white. Sprinkle on sesame seeds.

Place the cookies on a cookie sheet.

Bake the cookies in an oven for 15 minutes, until lightly brown on top.

Makes 2 dozen cookies.

Welcoming Spring

People always have celebrated the beginning of spring as a joyful time of new babies, new crops, flowering plants, and longer days of sunshine. Thousands of years ago, people held a **festival** to honor the goddess of spring. Her name was Estre. The name for Easter may have come from this goddess. People celebrated Estre's day by giving each other gifts, such as eggs and sweets. Today the Easter holiday is celebrated from Friday to Sunday. Friday is called Good Friday. It is a quiet day when Christians go to church to remember the death of Jesus. Some Christians celebrate Holy Saturday. On Easter Sunday, Christians joyfully celebrate when Jesus rose from the dead.

Easter is celebrated in the springtime, when flowers bloom, babies are born in nature, and winter finally ends.

7

Lent

The festival of Easter actually begins 40 days before Easter Sunday. The time during these 40 days is known as Lent. **Traditionally** it is a time of **fasting**, **sacrifice**, and prayer. During Lent, some Christians do not eat meat or foods made with butter, sugar, or eggs. Pretzels were invented by a young **monk** in A.D. 610. He was preparing a special bread for Lent. The bread, which later became known as a pretzel, did not have any milk or eggs in it, so that it could be eaten throughout Lent. Pretzels were made in the shape of arms crossed in prayer. The monk gave them as treats to children who recited their prayers.

Singing Easter hymns is an important part of celebrating Easter. These children sing in a church choir.

Easter Sunday

Good Friday is the last day of Lent. Because this is a sad day of **mourning**, many churches remove decorations from their **altars** and turn off the lights in the church. Easter Sunday is a day of celebration. Lights are turned back on, candles are lit, and the church is filled with flowers. People come to church wearing new clothes to **symbolize** the new beginning that Easter celebrates. The church service is joyful and full of music. After church, people gather with friends and family to feast and to be together. Many families around the world decorate their Easter dinner tables with flowers and eat holiday foods.

Left: This Easter Sunday table has lots of delicious foods, including colored eggs, hot chocolate, and chocolate candy.

Eggs, a Symbol of Easter

Eggs are a very old symbol of life and birth. It is believed that in very **ancient** times, people were amazed to see live baby chicks coming out of an egg. Today eggs are part of the holiday table. Some are hard-boiled, then dyed with food coloring. Others might be chocolate or candy eggs. In America, children usually get both hard-boiled eggs, and candy or chocolate eggs in their Easter baskets. Children in France have egg-rolling contests. The child whose egg rolls the farthest without breaking is the winner.

In Washington D.C., there is a very famous egg-rolling contest on the lawn of the White House on the Monday after Easter.

Right: Children come from all over the country to take part in the Easter egg-rolling contests on the White House lawn.

12

Beautiful Easter Eggs

In ancient times, people dyed eggs and gave them to one another as gifts in the beginning of spring. Today Christians around the world decorate eggs at Easter. In Greece, people boil eggs and then dye them red. In Germany, people poke a small hole in both ends of uncooked eggs and blow out the insides, leaving only the shell. Then they decorate the eggs and hang them on Easter trees. Polish and **Ukrainian** people make very beautiful eggs by creating designs with hot wax and a special dye. They peel off the wax to show an interesting design. In America, deviled eggs are a favorite way to eat hard-boiled eggs.

This basket of Easter foods includes Ukranian dyed eggs and breads.

14

Deviled Eggs

You will need:

4 hard-boiled eggs

¼ teaspoon (1.2 ml)
   salt

½ teaspoon (2.5 ml)
   dry mustard

1 teaspoon (5 ml)
   pickle relish

1 tablespoon (15 ml)
   melted butter

Paprika

How to do it:

Crack the eggshells of the cooked eggs and peel them.

Slice each egg in half.

Carefully remove the yolks from the whites and place the
   yolks in a bowl.

Place egg white halves on a plate.

Mash yolks with a fork.

Add remaining ingredients to yolks and mash.

Use a teaspoon to add yolk mixture to egg white halves.

Sprinkle each deviled egg with paprika.

The Easter Rabbit

The rabbit is another old symbol of birth and spring. When people began to celebrate Easter, rabbits were symbols that celebrated new life. Today children might find rabbits made of sugar or chocolate in the Easter baskets. Some people bake bunny-shaped cakes or cookies for Easter. Many children believe that the Easter bunny leaves Easter baskets or Easter eggs for them on the night of Holy Saturday. On Easter Sunday, children hunt for eggs and other treats that the Easter bunny might have left for them during the night. In Germany, children search in gardens and yards for eggs said to have been laid by the "Easter Hare." Egg nests made of coconut and jelly beans make delicious Easter treats.

Candy Easter Egg Nests

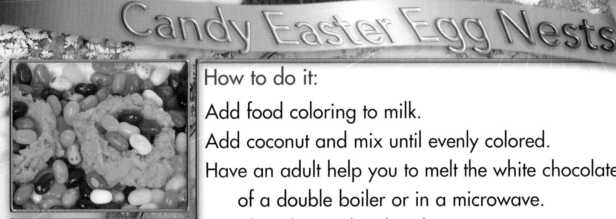

How to do it:

Add food coloring to milk.

Add coconut and mix until evenly colored.

Have an adult help you to melt the white chocolate in the top of a double boiler or in a microwave.

Mix chocolate with colored coconut.

Form into four balls and place on waxed paper.

Press the center of each ball to form a bird's nest.

Let nests set for an hour.

Fill the centers with jellybeans.

You will need:

2 drops of green food coloring

½ teaspoon (2.5 ml) of milk

1⅓ cups (315 ml) flaked coconut

6 ounces (170 g) of white chocolate

½ pound (227 g) jelly beans

Easter Breads and Meats

Easter Sunday meals often include meat, as well as sweet breads made with butter, eggs, honey, and cream. In Great Britain and in the United States, many people eat hot cross buns on Good Friday. These are sweet rolls with a cross made of icing on their tops. The cross is a symbol of Christ. People used to think that Good Friday hot cross buns had magical powers to heal sick people. Sailors would take Good Friday hot cross buns on journeys to keep them safe from shipwrecks. Christians around the world also eat lamb on Easter. Lamb is a symbol of Jesus Christ, who is also known as the Lamb of God. Ham is also a favorite meat eaten at Easter. One way to serve ham is in a rich and delicious ham and cheese pie.

Ham and Cheese Pie

You will need:

1 unbaked piecrust
6 strips of bacon
2 thin slices of boiled ham
6 ounces (170 g) thinly sliced Swiss cheese
4 eggs
1 tablespoon (15 ml) flour
½ tablespoon (7.4 ml) salt
Dash of nutmeg
1 cup (237 ml) milk
1 cup (237 ml) light cream

How to do it:

Have an adult help you to set an oven at 375 degrees Fahrenheit (191 °C).

Sauté bacon until crisp. Drain on paper towels.

Break bacon into halves.

Cut ham and cheese into strips the same size as bacon.

Place bacon, ham, and cheese into the unbaked piecrust. Have pieces overlap.

Beat eggs. Stir in the flour, salt, nutmeg, milk, and light cream.

Place egg mixture into a saucepan. Cook over medium heat.

Stir until mixture coats the spoon.

Pour mixture into pie crust.

Bake for 40 minutes.

Easter Around the World

Christians all around the world celebrate Easter. In Greece, Orthodox Christians attend their dark and silent churches on Saturday night just before midnight. At midnight, the lights are turned on in the church, candles are lit, and people sing in celebration of the rebirth of Jesus Christ. In some countries, people begin their Easter celebration at dawn. They may sit on a hilltop or a mountain so that they can watch the sun rise. In many countries in Europe, people bring eggs and other food to church to be blessed. Then they take the food home and begin their Easter feast, which may last all day.

Left: *The candlelight is from people celebrating Easter at a holy place in Israel.* Right: *A Christian celebrates Easter.*

Easter Is Celebration

Many religions have holidays that celebrate the coming of spring. For Christian people, Easter is their holiday that celebrates spring and new life. All over the world, Christian people celebrate Easter with special church services, Easter parades, and wonderful meals with their families and friends. In New York City, there is a famous parade on Easter. People dress up in fancy clothes. Many wear beautiful or unusually decorated hats, and they walk along New York City's Fifth Avenue. No matter where in the world Easter is celebrated, it is always a time of beautiful flowers, wonderful food, and joyful celebration.

Glossary

altars (AHL-terz) Table or stone used in religious ceremonies.

ancient (AYN-chent) Very old; from a long time ago.

celebrate (SEH-luh-brayt) To observe a special time or day with festive activities.

Christian (KRIS-chun) The name of both the religion and the people who follow the teachings of Jesus Christ.

fasting (FAS-ting) Going without food, or certain kinds of food.

festival (FES-tih-vul) A time of rejoicing or feasting, often in memory of an important person or event.

monk (MUNK) A religious man who lives and works in a monastery.

mourning (MOR-ning) Showing sadness over the death of something.

Orthodox (OR-thuh-doks) A kind of Christian religion that is practiced mainly in Greece and in Eastern Europe.

rebirth (ree-BERTH) To be spiritually born again.

sacrifice (SA-krih-fys) To give up something for an ideal or a belief.

symbolize (SIM-buh-lyz) To stand for something important.

traditionally (truh-DIH-shuh-nuh-lee) A way of doing something that is passed down through the years.

Ukrainian (yu-CRAY-nee-un) People from Ukraine, a country in Eastern Europe.

23

Index

Web Sites

www.cs.unc.edu/%7Eyakowenk/pysanky/index.html
www.execpc.com/%7Etmuth/easter/holiday.htm
www.wilstar.com/holidays/easter.htm

24